Johnny Depp

AN ILLUSTRATED STORY

DAVID BASSOM

HAMLYN

The author would like to thank the following individuals for their assistance and support: Julian Brown; Tessa, Michael and Danny O'Brien; Kathleen Cunningham; Anwar Brett; Mike Campbell-Montgomery; David Richardson; Jerry Cheung; Mike Cracknell; and of course, Bridget Cunningham.

Photographic Acknowledgements
Front cover: **Ronald Grant Archive.**
Back cover top: **Corbis/Everett**
bottom, left to right: **Ronald Grant Archive, Ronald Grant Archive, Aquarius Picture Library.**

All Action 44 centre left, 77, /Graham Attwood 76 top left, /Foto Blitz 69, /Jean Cummings 64 bottom, /Robin Kennedy 48, /P.A.G. 12 top left.

Aquarius Picture Library 37 centre right, 38/9, 68, /Cesare Bonazza 14 top left, 65, 80, /Bruce W. Talamon 70 bottom left, /Bruce W.Talamon 70 top.

Corbis/Everett 2/3, 11, 17, 19 bottom right, 21 top right, 23 bottom right, 28/9, 29 bottom right, 29 top right, 31, 36 bottom left, 37 bottom right, 47 bottom right, 47 top right, 52, 53, 54/5, 54 top left, 54 bottom left, 60, 66/7, 74 top left, 78/9, /Bruce W. Talamon 71 bottom right.

Ronald Grant Archive 42/3, /1990 Universal 27, /1990 Universal City Studios 26/7.

Katz 36 top, 46/7, 50/1, 58/9, 62, /Deborah Feingold 19 top right, /Marty Katz 64 top left, /Gerardo Somoza 64 centre left.

Kobal Collection 6/7, 13 , 20 bottom left, 32/3, 34, 35, 38, 45, 47 centre right, 56 bottom left, 60/1, /Henny Garfunkel 24/5. Photofest 8, 16/17, 20 top, 22 bottom left, 22 top left, 23 top right, 37 top right, 56 top left, 74 bottom left, 74/5, /Bruce Birmelin 44 bottom left, /Christine Parry 72/3, /Bruce W. Talamon 71 top right.

Pictorial Press 12 centre left, 30 top left, 57 top right, 63 top right, 63 bottom right, /SF/Zuffante 57 bottom right.

Retna /Bruce Birmelin 44 top left, /Larry Busacca 12 bottom left, /E.J Camp/ Onyx 9 right, /Bill Davila 76 bottom left, /Harrison Funk 21 bottom right, /Henny Garfunkel 29 centre right, /Steve Granitz 30 bottom left, /Leon Lecash 10 left, /Marion Samuels 15.

Rex Features 14 bottom left, 40/1, 43, 54 centre left, /Dave Lewis 49.

Executive Editor Julian Brown
Assistant Editor Karen O'Grady
Production Controller Melanie Frantz
Picture Research Maxine McCaghy
Design Steve Byrne

First published in Great Britain in 1996
by Hamlyn, an imprint of Reed Consumer Books
Limited, Michelin House, 81 Fulham Road,
London SW3 6RB
and Auckland, Melbourne, Singapore and Toronto

ISBN 0 600 59091 7

A catalogue record for this book is available from
the British Library

Produced by Mandarin Offset
Printed in Hong Kong

Johnny Depp

▶▶

1

BORN TO BE WILD

Born To Be Wild

Above and right: **Depp successfully abandoned his teen heart-throb tag by playing a series of weird and wonderful movie roles**

gun-slinging four-year tour of duty in the crime-infested streets (and schools) of Vancouver in *21 Jump Street,* the actor has demonstrated a flair for comedy (*Cry-Baby, Ed Wood*), a gift for mime (*Edward Scissorhands, Benny & Joon*), a penchant for offbeat drama (*Arizona Dream, What's Eating Gilbert Grape?*) and a readiness for romance (*Don Juan de Marco*)

Depp has also managed to bring some of cinema's most unusual creations to life with supreme confidence and conviction; few actors would even consider trying to play such a diverse range of characters, which includes Don Juan DeMarco (the world's greatest lover), Edward Scissorhands (the man-made tragic outcast), Wade 'Cry-Baby' Walker (the archetypal troubled teen) and Ed Wood (the angora-loving non-director).

Depp's unconventional, weird but wonderful big-screen roles enabled him to eradicate memories of his teen idol status and earned him no less than three prestigious Golden Globe Award nominations.

Besides being an extremely popular performer, Depp is highly respected within the film industry. The actor's presence in a project (no matter how offbeat or quirky) is widely perceived as a hallmark of quality, whilst almost all of the actors he has worked with have commended Depp for his skill, enthusiasm, dedication and raw energy.

As well as being regularly touted as the successor to James Dean, the actor is frequently said to have the screen appeal of Marilyn Monroe and the versatility of Dustin Hoffman. In any case, Depp has acquitted himself admirably alongside the likes of Marlon Brando, Martin Landau, Christopher Walken, Faye Dunaway and Jerry Lewis, and been praised by some of the world's most distinguished (and most idiosyncratic) directors, including Tim Burton, Oliver Stone, John Waters and Jim Jarmusch.

Depp's unusual film roles and his wild off-screen antics have inevitability led to him being branded a 'teen idol-turned-madman' by the media on numerous occasions. While the list is virtually endless, the actor's most common tag lines include, 'Mad, Bad and Beautiful', 'The Crown Prince of Kooky', 'Cinema's Dysfunctional Hunk' and 'The Pin-Up With a Bunch of Hang-Ups'!

Despite his desire for privacy, Depp just cannot keep out of the headlines and the actor is probably as well known for his colourful love-life, tattoos and hotel-trashing misadventures (which have earned him a place in a prison cell on more than one occasion) as for his marvellous performances.

In much the same way that the public have been intrigued by his unconventional real-life escapades, money-minded movie moguls have been perplexed by Depp's reluctance to become involved with their so-called 'commercial projects' and his preoccupation with little-seen labours of love. Whilst Depp scored two modest box office hits with *Edward Scissorhands* and *Don Juan De Marco,* the actor has yet to topline a true box-office blockbuster and turned down several lucrative offers, including the lead roles in *Speed* and *Legends of the Fall* which helped elevate his contemporaries Keanu Reeves and Brad Pitt to superstar status. Ironically, Depp's most commercial vehicle to date, the action-packed thriller *Nick of Time*, proved to be a box office bomb.

However, Depp has repeatedly stated that he prefers to work on projects that he finds appealing rather than sure-fire money spinners and has made it clear that his experience of being a 'teen idol' has put him off the idea of becoming a global superstar.

The actor has no regrets over his post-*Jump Street* decisions and is untroubled by the thought that he might have sacrificed his commercial appeal for artistic merit. Furthermore, the actor hopes to extend his talents as he moves towards writing and directing. Thus, if virtue is its own reward, then Johnny Depp is truly a rich man.

Given Depp's phenomenal success as an actor, it's amazing to think that he originally travelled to Hollywood to pursue his

Born To Be Wild

Top: Depp at the 1995 Cannes Film Festival with musician Neil Young and director Jim Jarmusch to promote *Dead Man*

Centre: Out on the town with another of Hollywood's famous hellraisers, Charlie Sheen

Above: Backstage at the Fez, New York City, with girlfriend Kate Moss and Johnny Cash

Opposite: Depp spoofed his teen idol image as Wade Walker in *Cry Baby*

career as a musician. Born in Owensboro, Kentucky, on 9 June 1963, John Christopher Depp, II was the youngest of four children (he has two sisters and one brother).

During the first few years of his life, Depp's upbringing was straightforward and unglamorous, and he had little connection with showbusiness; his father worked as a city engineer, whilst his mother (from whom the future-actor gained his part-Cherokee ancestry) was a waitress. Some years later, when he was asked what he had inherited from his parents, Depp quipped: 'Chain-smoking and insanity.'

Johnny Depp's childhood memories are as unusual as you would expect from such an eccentric talent. His earliest recollections are, believe it or not, of his grandmother's toe-nails! ('I don't know why, but I can just remember seeing them,' he later revealed. 'They were like cashews.')

He also remembers being attacked by an enraged swarm of bees after unwisely shaking their hive and that his childhood idol was the American pioneer Daniel Boone.

Depp became aware of his own eccentricity at an early stage of his life. 'I remember feeling a freak when I was about five,' he said. 'I looked at other kids and had weird feelings about being the odd one out.'

In 1970, Depp's family decided to relocate to Miramar, Florida, where they lived near his uncle, a local preacher. During the next few years, the Depps moved house nearly thirty times and Johnny began his pursuit of the wild life.

By 1974, he was apparently known as a drug user, vandal and thief by his peers and was suspended from school for flashing his buttocks at one of his teachers.

The following year, Depp began his life-long love affair with rock 'n' roll. When his cousins' gospel group visited his home, the young delinquent played an electric guitar for the first time and became 'obsessed' with the instrument, until his mother bought him a guitar for $25. He then spent a year learning how to play.

▶▶

Born To Be Wild

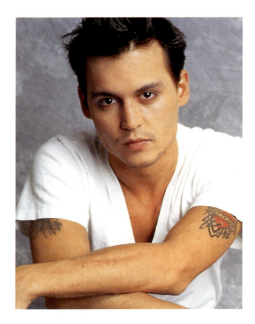

Top: Depp became interested in the art of tattooing at an early age

Above: Following his parents' divorce, Johnny was raised by his mother, Betty Sue

Opposite: A self-taught guitarist, Depp moved to Los Angeles with the Kids in 1983 in the hope of becoming a world-famous musician

Around the same time, Depp became fascinated with tattoos following his somewhat foolhardy decision to carve his initials on his arm. Despite the pain, he was intrigued and subsequently had tattoos engraved on his left and right biceps. 'I've always respected tattooing as an art form,' he explained many years later. 'I always did it as part of an art that your wear, as a kind of journal. Your body is your journal.'

Depp suffered further physical injury when a friend decided to mimic a fire-breathing act he had seen at a circus. The pair of would-be circus performers tied a cloth around a tree and set fire to it, and then spat mouthfuls of petrol towards the flames! Depp's face caught fire as a result, but luckily he suffered only minor burns.

In 1975, the self-taught guitarist made his public debut with his first garage band, Flame, who became more famous for their distinctive T-Shirts (plain white garments which had the word 'Flame' imaginatively adorned on them) than for their music. Depp, who usually sported 'long and shaggy' hair and T-Shirts as a teenager, soon learned that the bandmembers – despite their talent – were not short of female fans, and subsequently became a romantic heart-throb in the eyes of many local girls.

Depp was 15 years old when his parents divorced and following the break-up, he was raised by his mother, Betty Sue, and his two sisters. The young man would later attribute this period of his life to explain his appreciation of the opposite sex.

Shortly after the split, Depp decided to drop out of high school. 'I was bored with it,' he subsequently explained. 'All I had on my mind was playing the guitar and dropping out.' The teenage rebel felt that his teachers held little hope for his future and more or less expected him to end up in jail as a drug addict. 'I think the teachers thought I was a weirdo and they didn't know how to deal with me,' Depp recalled. 'What they didn't realise was that I didn't know how to deal with myself.'

Looking back on his decision to leave school, Depp admitted that it was a mistake. 'High School's a breeze,' he stated. 'I mean, yeah, you've got pressures and you've got the tough guy picking on you and you've got the girl you love and she doesn't look at you. But compared to life, it's a real breeze man.'

With school out forever, Johnny was free to pursue his career as a musician and played the rock 'n' roll clubs across Florida as a member of a new band, the Kids. The under-age guitarist quickly adapted to life as a night-owl and would only be allowed into venues to play on the strict condition that he stayed away from their bars. On average, the Kids would take $2,100 a night, of which Depp would earn $25.

During the following few years, the Kids had a great deal of regional success. They opened for the likes of the B-52s and Talking Heads, and in 1981, played two shows with legendary rocker Iggy Pop. After one of the gigs, Depp saw the rock star and suddenly started to scream abuse at him. 'I don't know why, because I always idolised him,' Depp later explained 'And he walked over to me and just looked at me, and I thought he was going to kill me. And he said, "You little turd." And he walked away.'

Ironically, when Depp discussed the event with Iggy Pop some nine years later, when the pair were shooting *Cry-Baby*, Iggy told him, 'I was probably in the same condition as you, maybe worse.'

In 1983, Depp married Lori Anne Allison, a 25-year-old make-up artist. The marriage ended within two years and Depp later said of their relationship, 'It was a very strong bond but I'm not sure I was in love.'

Within months of Depp's wedding, the Kids got the 'big break' they had been waiting for when they were approached by Hollywood music impresario Don Ray, who offered to manage the group. Once their contracts had been finalised, Depp and his fellow Kids left for Los Angeles, where they believed that fame and fortune awaited the young rockers.

2

FROM ELM STREET TO JUMP STREET

Depp's talent was recognised during his very first audition

Despite their success in clubs across Florida, the Kids were unprepared for what awaited them in the entertainment capital of the world, Hollywood. With so many up-and-coming bands vying for attention, Johnny Depp and his fellow musicians soon realised that life in LA was going to be tougher than they thought, and decided that they needed to find day jobs to support their musical careers. Depp soon found employment as a biro pen telesalesman and earned around $100 a week. However, job satisfaction eluded the would-be wild-man rock legend.

'We had to rip people off,' he later said. 'We'd say they'd been chosen by so-and-so in their area to receive a grandfather clock . . . They would order $500 worth of these f***ing things and we would send them a cheap grandfather clock. It was horrible.'

During their first months in Hollywood, the Kids played a few shows and generally received a good response. They supported the likes of Billy Idol and the Bus Boys, but unfortunately, gigs were few and far between and the band members became increasingly dependent on their 'supplementary' incomes to pay the bills.

As time went on, Depp began to despair at his role in the world of telemarketing and was seriously thinking about his options for a new day job when his wife, Lori Anne Allison, introduced him to her close friend, Nicolas Cage, the aspiring actor who was destined to find fame in such films as *Peggy Sue Got Married, Raising Arizona* and *Leaving Las Vegas*. Upon hearing the details of Depp's predicament, Nicolas Cage sent the unemployed musician to see his agent, who in turn sent Depp to audition for a role in New Line's low-budget horror flick, *A Nightmare on Elm Street.*

Arriving at the casting call, the dark-haired, shy and retiring musician felt that he had little chance of winning the role of Glen, who was described in the film's script as 'a big blonde jock football player'. However, despite his lack of experience or training, Depp's reading overwhelmed the film's director, veteran horrormeister Wes Craven, and New Line's casting agent Annette Benson. Craven later commented that Depp displayed 'sort of a James Dean attraction – that quiet charisma that none of the other actors had,' and knew that he had to use the unknown performer. Consequently, the musician-turned-actor was offered the part a mere five hours later, and the role was rewritten by Craven to suit him.

An innovative and genuinely terrifying take on the slice 'n' dice genre, *A Nightmare on Elm Street* proved to be a surprise hit at the box office and spawned no less than six sequels (with a seventh in pre-production) as well as a weekly TV series. As far as Depp was concerned, his appearance in the film provided an effortless screen debut; as Glen, one of the teenagers haunted by wise-cracking dream-master Freddy Krueger (Robert Englund), the biggest challenge was to look scared when his character was sucked into his bed to meet an untimely (and extremely gory) end!

Although the film launched the Freddy Krueger phenomenon, it didn't make stars of any of its cast; even the most-die hard *Elm Street* fan couldn't argue that Heather Langencamp, Robert Englund, Amanda Wyss et al became household names. Depp himself never held much hope for his screen debut and so wasn't disappointed by its impact on his career. 'What kind of reviews can you get opposite Freddy Krueger?' he later explained. 'Johnny Depp was good as the boy who died?'

However, in the long term, *A Nightmare on Elm Street* was set to have a massive affect on Depp's future. Upon receiving his pay cheque, the part-time thespian was

Top: **After working as a biro pen salesman, Johnny Depp turned to acting to support his musical career**

Above: **Depp made his inauspicious acting debut as doomed teenager Glen in *A Nightmare on Elm Street***

Above: After starring in *Private Resort*, Depp decided to take his acting career more seriously and honed his skills at the Loft Studio

shocked by how lucrative acting could be, even at the bottom of the ladder. 'It was amazing to me that someone wanted to pay me that much money, which was just union scale,' he stated.

A few months later, Depp landed his first co-starring role in the coarse comedy *Private Resort,* a sequel to the equally dreadful *Private Lessons* and *Private School.* Best described as a imbecilic cross between *Police Academy* and *Baywatch, Private Resort* follows the romantic adventures of lust-struck teenagers Jack (Rob Morrow) and Ben (Johnny Depp) at an expensive Miami resort. Whilst Jack finds himself in drag and on the run from a dangerous jewel thief known only as the Maestro (Hector Elizondo), Ben pursues virtually every woman he happens to set eyes on, including Patti (Emily Longstreth) and Bobby Sue (Leslie Easterbrook).

Despite the efforts of a sterling cast, *Private Resort* is an unmitigated celluloid catastrophe. Cliched, offensive and instantly forgettable, the dimwitted non-comedy is a complete embarrassment for Depp and easily the worst project he has

ever been associated with. In fact, probably the only thing of interest concerning *Private Resort* is the way Depp's portrayal of the lust-obsessed Ben compares with his work in *Don Juan De Marco* exactly ten years later.

Once work on the film wrapped, Depp decided that the time had come to carefully consider his future. Regardless of its artistic merit, *Private Resort* had not only provided him with a good salary but also with a free holiday in Miami (where most of the film was shot), whilst his musical (non-) career had become just a distraction. Aware that if he trained as an actor, he might be cast in better projects, he began to consider the possibility of attending drama school.

After a great deal of soul searching, Depp decided that he wanted to concentrate on his career as an actor and abandon – at least for the time being – his hopes of becoming a rock star. Much to his colleagues' dismay, he left the Kids (who were subsequently forced to disband) and studied acting at the celebrated Loft Studio.

Depp also finalised his divorce from his wife, Lori Anne Allison, in 1985. By all accounts, it was a mutual and amicable split,

From Elm Street
To Jump Street

and there was no acrimony or trauma surrounding separation proceedings. Shortly afterwards, Depp began dating Sherilyn Fenn, a young actress who would later find fame in the quirky TV series *Twin Peaks* and star in such films as *Boxing Helena* and *Three of Hearts.* After a few months, Fenn and Depp became engaged.

'He was my first real love,' she later said, 'and I think I was his first real engagement – of many.' The couple stayed together for three years until their whirlwind romance ended in a cloud of smoke.

Once he had graduated from the Loft Studio, Depp reluctantly decided that he would have to stay in Hollywood if he was to find work as an actor. He subsequently divided his time between Los Angeles and New York hotels, and repeated his dislike of Hollywood on several occasions: 'I live there because I have to,' he stated, 'but it's only a temporary roosting spot.'

The actor entered the auditions circuit and within a few weeks, landed a small role in *Slow Burn,* a routine thriller made for cable television starring Eric Roberts as a private investigator on the trail of an artist.

Although Depp wondered if his training had been a waste of time, his outlook changed when he learned about a possible role in the film *Platoon*: Oliver Stone's semi-autobiographical Vietnam War epic.

Inevitably, Depp felt completely terrified before the larger-than-life director, but managed to impress him in the audition. 'I read for him and he said, "Okay, I need you for ten weeks in the jungle"', the actor revealed 'It was a great experience.'

Shot on location in the Philippines, *Platoon* is a gruelling and uncompromising look at America's involvement in the Vietnam War, as seen through the eyes of naive volunteer Chris (Charlie Sheen, in a role based on Stone). In late 1967, the rookie soldier is assigned to a unit patrolling the Cambodian border and becomes caught between the platoon's three factions; the militaristic, flag-waving 'might is right' no-nonsense soldiers led by the battle-scarred Barnes (Tom Berenger); the pragmatic and war-weary veterans under the reluctant command of Elias (Willem Dafoe); and the drugged-out loners, concerned only with survival.

Platoon proved to be an impressive, if slightly provocative, hit at the box office and subsequently won an Oscar for Best Picture in 1987. Although Depp only had a minor supporting role as the group's interpreter, Lerner, the film nevertheless provided him with his first taste of 'real' acting. Consequently, Depp felt inspired by his experience with Oliver Stone and vowed to choose his future roles more carefully. He returned to the audition circuit and, in a reversal of fortune, joined a new band, the Rock City Angels, in order to supplement his income as an actor.

In 1987, Depp learned that Fox Television wanted him for role in *21 Jump Street,* a series co-created by Stephen J. Cannell (whose earlier shows include *The A-Team).* As far as Depp's agent was concerned, it was an incredible offer: the show would provide regular work, possible stardom and a guaranteed wage. It was the kind of thing that most actors have to wait several years for and work their way towards. Consequently, it came as something of a shock when Depp revealed that he had no intention of joining the show; the actor said that he didn't particularly like the

Top: Depp felt inspired whilst working on Oliver Stone's acclaimed Vietnam epic *Platoon.*

Above: After working as an actor to finance his musical career, Depp joined a new band, The Rock City Angels, to supplement his income as an actor

From Elm Street To Jump Street

Above: Depp originally turned down the prestigious lead role in *21 Jump Street* and was only persuaded to join the show's cast when his replacement, Jeff Yagher, was deemed unsuitable by its producers

Opposite: As Tom Hanson, a straight-laced cop forced to pose as a rebellious high school student, Depp became a reluctant television star and teen idol

idea of starring in yet another cop show, or the prospect of being tied to a project for several years. Against the advice of almost everyone around him, the virtually unknown and relatively inexperienced actor turned down the lucrative offer and the role was subsequently recast.

However, the *21 Jump Street* story was far from over. A mere month into production of the series, the producers reportedly decided that Depp's substitute, Jeff Yagher, wasn't convincing or suitably charismatic in the lead role and re-opened negotiations with Depp's agent. Aware that his client had been given a second chance at fame and wealth, Depp's agent refused to take no for an answer and desperately tried to convince him to accept the role.

Gradually, Depp began to reconsider his position: worthy roles were few and far between and *21 Jump Street* was one of the best projects he had been offered; most American TV series are short-lived and the average duration of a show is 13 episodes, so *Jump Street* might not have meant a long-term commitment; and veteran TV actor Frederick Forrest (an actor Depp admired) had signed to play his boss, Captain Jenko.

Ultimately, Depp decided to give *21 Jump Street* a shot and flew to Vancouver, Canada, to head a largely unknown cast, including Judy Hoffs, Peter DeLuise and Dustin Nguyen, for what he envisaged would be a six-month tour of duty.

Best described as a cross between *Hill Street Blues* and *Beverly Hills 90210*, *21 Jump Street* takes its name from the fictious Jump Street Unit, a top-secret special division of the force which uses young cops to go undercover and stop juvenile crime.

When it becomes clear that the criminal underworld won't take conservative young police officer Tom Hanson (Depp) seriously due to his 'baby-face', Hanson is forced to choose between taking a desk job or being reassigned to the newly-installed Jump Street Division. Under the command of their unorthodox chief, Captain Jenko (Forrest), the teen cops pose as troubled high school students to crack underage crime. *21 Jump Street* made its debut in Spring 1987 and, much to everyone's surprise, became an instant smash hit in the ratings.

During its first season, the show tackled such moral issues as child abuse, juvenile crime and AIDS, while Depp made an extremely charismatic, if somewhat conventional, leading man. Audience research showed that the show and its main character struck a chord with teenagers across America; young male viewers could relate to Hanson's rebellious behaviour and his action-packed heroics, whilst many young girls tuned in to see Depp in probably his coolest and most accessible role to date.

Unsurprisingly, therefore, *21 Jump Street* made Johnny Depp a star virtually overnight. Although the young performer felt that the show 'didn't have anything to do with acting,' he started to face unparalleled and relentless media attention within weeks of the show's debut.

Depp's face soon began to dominate the covers of teen magazines across America and he was subsequently voted one of the 'Ten Sexiest Bachelors in the Entertainment Industry' by *US* magazine, as well as being named as one of the 'Hot Faces of 1988' by *Rolling Stone* magazine.

For Depp, fame and the teen idol tag were something of a disaster. Although he had experienced minor recognition with the Kids, becoming a media sensation overnight was something else. Depp soon made it clear that he was horrified by all the interest surrounding him, as an actor in a TV show.

'I can't really understand why there should be all this interest in the private life of someone who basically sells lies for money,' he said. 'An actor is just an actor, after all.'

Depp soon became sick of his status as a teen heart-throb and stated, 'I don't see myself as a sex symbol' on numerous occasions. As the media spotlight intensified, Depp's fan mail increased tenfold and he was soon receiving up to 10,000 fan letters a month – including marriage proposals and underwear garments!

'All the strange fan mail gets a little weird sometimes,' he said. 'I'm just doing a job – acting. All the other stuff that comes with that can get uncomfortable.' The actor also learned that fame can be dangerous. 'I get attention from real psychos sometimes,' he explained. 'I've gotten death threats and there's a guy who thinks he is me.'

Depp's involvement with *21 Jump Street* was filled with irony: he initially agreed to star in the show believing that it would only run for half a season, but instead it became a runaway success; he wanted to do the show in order to work with Frederic Forrest, but the veteran actor left the series after six episodes; and he was looking for roles to develop his acting talent, but instead emerged as a star and teen idol.

To make matters worse, as *21 Jump Street's* popularity soared, the show became a victim of its own success. Fox executives, desperate that their fledgling network wouldn't offend any viewers or possible advertisers, ordered the show's producers to make the series 'less controversial and more conventional'. In effect, this meant that the show's more ambitious storylines were dropped and replaced by every routine cop/action/drama show cliche imaginable. Inevitably, *21 Jump Street* became the teenage equivalent of *The A-Team*.

Depp, who had been pleasantly surprised by the quality of some of the show's first season outings, swiftly sensed the change in format and increased his role in the creative process during the show's subsequent years.

However, when the press discovered that Depp would constantly question his character's motives and the show's moral outlook, he was immediately branded as a 'teen troublemaker'. Then, when Depp leaked storylines in an effort to illustrate how juvenile the show had become, he was judged to be a liability by the studio.

Despite his feelings about the show's rapidly dwindling artistic merit, *21 Jump Street* remained a huge hit with teenage audiences everywhere and even managed to spawn a spin-off series, *Booker,* which starred Richard Greico.

Finding himself trapped by a binding contract, Depp, the former drop-out, unfortunately now found that he could not leave high school no matter what he did.

During the show's third season (1988 to 89), Johnny Depp became engaged to Jennifer Gray, the star of *Dirty Dancing*, following the break-up of his three-year relationship with Sherilyn Fenn. His second engagement lasted only a year.

By 1989, Depp's salary had soared to $45,000 an episode ($1 million a year) and even more lucrative offers were coming his way. However, the actor refused to change his lifestyle or live up to his public image.

Apart from the hotel accommodation and rides provided by the studio, Depp had no apartment or car and his down 'n' dirty style of dress led to him being named as one of America's worst dressed young actors in a magazine poll.

Upon hearing the result, Depp stated, 'My goal is to be Number One worst dressed!' In March 1989, just prior to wrapping the thrid season of *21 Jump Street,* Depp was arrested and jailed for assault.

Unfulfilled and deeply unhappy, Johnny Depp wanted to escape the 'insanity' of his life as an American star and teen idol, and looked carefully for a project which could take his career in a new direction.

Above: Like Wade Walker in *Cry Baby*, Johnny Depp is no stranger to being on the wrong side of the law

When Waters revealed to the film's financial backers who he had in mind for its lead role, they immediately told him that Depp wouldn't do it. They informed the writer/ director that Depp had turned down a number of extremely lucrative film offers since *Jump Street* and it seemed unlikely that the reluctant teen idol would want to portray a teen idol on screen. Although they agreed to offer the actor a cool $1 million fee to star in the film, they believed he would never even think about the project.

Much to their surprise, Depp needed little persuasion to take the role and signed on the dotted line within days of receiving the script. For the actor realised that Wade 'Cry-Baby' Walker was in fact a spoof of the archetypal teen idol/rebel image and felt that it was a perfect vehicle for him to send up his public image and show audiences a different side of himself.

'It was the best script,' Depp later explained. 'It was the funniest . . . There were a lot of scripts where I would carry a gun,

Baby Love

Hearst, former porn star Traci Lords, Waters prodigy and future talk-show host Ricki Lake, former American heart-throb Troy Donahue and *Platoon's* Willem Dafoe.

During filming, the past kept catching up with Depp. The actor was lost for words when he was approached by one of his former school teachers, who casually asked for his autograph!

The high school drop out-turned-star was similarly amused when he was asked to present a Public Service anti-drugs campaign in which he was supposed to say, 'Hi, I'm Johnny Depp. Stay in school and graduate!' When Depp reminded the commercials' producers of his academic past, they swiftly dropped their request.

Best described as *Grease* and *Happy Days* on acid, *Cry-Baby* is an energetic and beautifully over the top satire of the early days of rock 'n' roll.

The film opens with petty hoodlum Wade 'Cry-Baby' Walker (Depp), realising that clean-cut, wholesome prom queen Allison (Amy Locane) 'only looks square' and invites her to hang out with his fellow 'Drapes'. When Allison elopes with Walker to see him sing at a redneck country club, her former 'square' friends follow seeking vengeance and start a fight which lands Cry-Baby a place in jail.

As Allison tries to choose between waiting for Walker or marrying his square rival, Milton (Darren E. Burrows), the Cry-Baby launches a daring (but rather stupid) escape bid before the prison barber can get his hands on the Drapes' distinctive locks.

While *Cry-Baby* didn't win any awards for its derivative and lazy storyline, it provided a wonderful opportunity for Depp to play against type and re-define his screen image. Consequently, the actor delivered a true *tour de force* and demonstrated the true scope of his ability for probably the first time in his career.

Depp delivers the film's deliberately over-the-top melodramatic dialogue with skillful ease and admirable conviction (he is particularly good in the scene when Walker explains how he earned the nickname Cry-Baby), whilst his marvellous miming and dynamic dancing are reminiscent of Elvis' finest performances.

kiss a girl, walk around corners and pose, and things like that . . . *Cry Baby* makes fun of all the stuff I sort of hate.'

Cry-Baby was shot on location in Baltimore (Waters' usual stomping ground) during the summer of 1989, whilst *21 Jump Street* was in its third season hiatus. As one would expect from the cult film-maker, the movie featured a suitably eclectic cast; besides showcasing America's hottest teen idol, it also starred veteran rocker Iggy Pop, reluctant criminal-turned-celebrity Patty

Top: Future chat show host Ricki Lake finds a familiar shoulder to lean on

Centre: Imprisoned and separated from Allison, Wade indulges some jailhouse rock

Above: The cast of *Cry Baby* are put through their paces by director John Waters (far right)

Baby Love

Top: A portrait of Wade 'Cry-Baby' Walker's family

Above: In 1990, Johnny Depp and Winona Ryder swiftly became one of Hollywood's hottest couples

Cry-Baby launched itself into American cinemas on 4 April 1990 and proved to be a modest financial success, thanks to Depp's undeniable screen appeal and his loyal fans.

Perhaps inevitably, when the film first opened, the actor was constantly asked to reveal what made him cry. Although he would normally reply that he wept whenever he was hurt, he soon became bored with the banal question and started to offer more off-beat answers. On one occasion he revealed, 'Sometimes I find myself crying when I'm in a restaurant and I see, say, an elderly woman eating. It's something to do with how human it is. And how necessary.'

Once shooting of *Cry-Baby* had wrapped, Depp returned to Vancouver for his fourth and final year of *21 Jump Street.* While the actor had secretly told John Waters that he believed the show would improve, Depp was once again unimpressed by its routine teenage cops 'n' robbers storylines and was overjoyed when he was released from his contract at the end of the season, after a total of 82 episodes.

Depp had no qualms about leaving the financial security of the show behind and was happy to pursue his film career, whilst Fox was confident that the series would continue to be a success without him. The fifth season of *21 Jump Street* began transmission in Fall 1990, and the show's ratings promptly plummeted. Consequently, the series was cancelled the following spring.

With *Jump Street* behind him and *Cry-Baby* slowly erasing his image as a teen idol, Depp hoped that he would no longer be the focus of media attention. However, he remained in the headlines thanks to his relationship with Hollywood starlet Winona Ryder, who found fame and acclaim in such films as *Heathers* and *Beetlejuice.*

Depp and Ryder first met through a mutual friend, Josh, and became an item shortly after. While Ryder expected that Depp would be a 'jerk', she felt that he was actually 'really, really shy', and the pair swiftly discovered that they had a lot of things in common; during their very first meeting, it became clear that they both had a genuine love for J. D. Salinger and the soundtrack album of 'The Mission'. They later discovered that they shared a mutual love of the offbeat and that neither had a home they could call their own. As a result, when Depp moved in with her, he actually began to stay at Ryder's hotel apartment!

Although Depp's reputation as a multi-engaged romeo preceded him, Ryder made it clear that she was not bothered by anything that happened in the past. 'I don't have a problem with it, we have a very stable relationship . . . We have a connection on a much deeper level.' Depp himself often said that he loved Ryder 'more than anything in the world' and decided to have a third tatoo proclaiming 'Winona Forever', engraved on his bicep to reassure her about their future together. The actor later quipped that he decided on a tattoo rather than an engagement ring because 'you can't lose a tatoo down a drain.'

Rather than being impressed, Ryder was shocked by his gesture of undying devotion. 'I kept thinking it was going to wash off,' she later revealed. 'I couldn't believe it was real. I mean, it's a big thing. It's so permanent.'

Depp and Ryder became one of Hollywood's hottest couples and their relationship was constantly under the media spotlight. When the actress withdrew from Francis Ford Coppola's *The Godfather Part III,* the rumour mill went into overdrive; although she was actually suffering from exhaustion and merely needed a break from work, some tabloids claimed that she was pregnant, whilst others suggested that Depp had begged her not to leave him alone during the making of the film.

Shortly after *The Godfather* fiasco, Ryder committed herself to a project in which she destined to co-star with her boyfriend. And if *Cry-Baby* was an unexpected vehicle for Johnny Depp, then *Edward Scissorhands* was a wholly unique outing for the former-teen idol.

4

SHEAR PERFECTION

Shear Perfection

Depp cut an unforgettable cinematic figure as Edward Scissorhands

Above: Edward (Johnny Depp) shows that his metal shears for hands do have their usefulness at barbecues

Opposite: With scissors for hands, Edward's every action is potentially lethal – even scratching his own face

One of the most original, evocative and touching films of the Nineties, *Edward Scissorhands* began life as a sketch from the pen of an aspiring animator attending the California Arts Institute. The artist's name was Tim Burton. During his years as an Disney animator, Burton began to envisage his curious creation as the lead character in a contemporary fairy tale and slowly developed his own storyline, elements of which reflected his childhood feeling of being an outsider in a crazy world.

'I was always intrigued by the images and ideas of fairy tales, but I never related specifically to them,' Burton explained. 'The idea with this is to take the themes and the ideas of those and just contemporise it a bit more, and hopefully make the link between real life and fairy tale a bit closer.'

In 1982, Burton made his directorial debut with *Vincent,* a seven-minute animated feature voiced by the legendary horror star Vincent Price. After directing his second film, *Frankenweenie,* he helmed his first live-action film, *Pee-Wee's Big Adventure.* When the zany comedy became a surprise hit in summer 1985, Burton was commissioned to make the weird 'n' wacky horror comedy *Beetlejuice*.

Whilst the film was in pre-production, the director had a business lunch with writer Caroline Thompson (who would later write the big screen adaptations of *The Addams Family* and *Black Beauty*). Realising that they shared the same outlook on storytelling and film-making, Burton showed her his sketch of *Edward Scissorhands* and outlined his plans for the movie.

'Tim had this brilliant image and no home for him,' she said. 'The minute he said to me, "It's about a guy who's got scissors for hands", bang, I knew the story . . . It was so resonant and so powerful and such a clear expression of feelings that it just set the whole thing off. The story is about not being able to touch anything, about feeling that everything you touch turns to tatters. It's about being awkward.'

Burton hired Thompson out of his own pocket to write a screenplay whilst he toiled behind the camera on *Beetlejuice*. When the film became his second surprise hit at the box office, Warners Bros. offered him the chance to helm their highly prestigious (and extremely troubled) big-budget, star-studded comic-strip adventure, *Batman*. Against the odds, *Batman* proved to be a phenomenally successfully (and incredibly over-hyped) adventure, and gave Burton the clout to bring *Edward Scissorhands* to the screen.

Or so you might think. Amazingly enough, Warner executives branded the storyline 'uncommercial' and declined the opportunity to produce it. Undeterred, Burton subsequently pitched the project to other studios, and it was swiftly picked up by 20th Century Fox, who offered the director a relatively paltry $18 million to bring his bizarre fantasy to the screen.

Once the film's funding had been secured, Burton and his co-producer, Denise Di Novi, turned their attention to

Top: Edward demonstrates one of his unique talents to a class of school children

Above: Edward Scissorhands' director Tim Burton discusses a scene with his friend and mentor, Vincent Price

casting. Almost immediately, the pair discovered that the script divided actors into two camps: they either loved or hated it.

Academy Award-winner Dianne Wiest (*Hannah and Her Sisters, Parenthood*) was among those who fell into the former group, and signed up almost immediately, as did Burton's idol and patron Vincent Price, who agreed to make a brief cameo as Edward's 'father', The Inventor.

Another of Burton's earliest signings was Winona Ryder, who had won his undying admiration for her portrayal of Lydia, the teenager with a special link with the Netherworld, in *Beetlejuice.* Ryder was delighted to work with the visionary director again on *Edward Scissorhands.*

'It's unlike any movie that's ever been made,' she said. 'It's just a completely original, modern-day fairy tale, and it's sort of timeless in a way.'

The most difficult aspect of all, though, was casting the title role. At the request of

Fox, the part was first offered to the world's leading box office draw, Tom Cruise.

Although Burton believed that he 'wouldn't even consider' the film, he was surprised when Cruise said that he would be interested in the role provided that the film was given a Disney-style happy ending. Unsurprisingly, Burton refused to compromise his vision, and negotiations collapsed.

Future Academy Award winner Tom Hanks and Robert Downey, Jr. (*Chances Are, Chaplin Air America*) were among those who declined the offbeat role before Depp was invited to meet with Burton to discuss the project. Unlike many of his contemporaries, Depp was truly excited at the prospect of starring in such a unique, challenging and unconventional movie.

'I thought the script was one of the best things I'd ever read, so of course I would have jumped at the opportunity to play him,' he explained. 'Because Edward is not Human, and not a robot, I didn't think that he

Shear Perfection

Jump Street, suddenly began to worry that the young actor would make Edward 'over the top and flamboyant'. Fortunately, when he viewed the first day's footage, Burton was 'amazed' by the actor's 'internal, simple style of acting'. During the making of the film Burton realised that he was not the only member of the cast and crew for whom *Edward Scissorhands* had special meaning.

'Johnny's own life mirrors the movie's theme; he's supposed to be this sexy *21 Jump Street* idol, yet he's so far removed from that' Burton remarked. 'There's a sadness about being perceived as something quite different from what you are inside. It gives him the sense of isolation he used so well in his performance.'

Edward Scissorhands was shot during the summer of 1990, and the cast spent seven weeks filming on location in a four-year-old housing estate in Lan O'Lakes, central Florida. In typically wacky fashion for Burton, no less than 45 of the estate's 50 houses were painted in an array of pastel colours and given minor face-lifts to create a 'timeless, archetypal suburb'.

In order to transform himself into Edward, Depp spent two hours in make-up each day and soon learned that wearing his character's all-in-one black leather costume and scissor gloves could be difficult in Florida's 100 degree temperatures.

'The costume Johnny had to wear was really frustrating because he couldn't do anything all day once he got it on,' explained Ryder. 'He couldn't scratch himself and he couldn't touch anything. He was going nuts.'

Futhermore, the compulsive coffee-drinker understandably dreaded the prospect of going to the bathroom whilst wearing his Scissorhands. 'I learnt to ignore my bladder,' he later quipped.

Beside the practical difficulties, Depp felt *Edward Scissorhands* was the hardest role he had ever played, and was wracked with self-doubt about his performance. It was only through the support of his co-stars Dianne Wiest, Alan Arkin and Vincent Price that he managed to stay focused on his work. 'They came to me when I was really doubting what I was doing and how I was doing,' Depp explained. 'And they said that I knew what I was doing. That I wasn't wrong.'

Top and centre: **Edward's gift for hairdressing soon makes him a local celebrity**

Above: **Depp spent two months learning how to use Edward's 12-inch long scissorhands**

would talk a lot. He would cut through everything and have the most honest, pure answer with all the clarity in the world.'

Aware that *Edward Scissorhands* was a man of few words but many emotions, Depp studied footage of Charlie Chaplin to learn about silent expressive acting techniques and body movements. He also spent two months learning how to use the 12 inch long scissor gloves, created by Academy Award-winning special effects designer Stan Winston and moulded from a special plastic.

'At first it felt strange working with the hands, but I got to where it felt pretty natural,' Depp said. 'It was important to me that I found, like Edward does in the movie, not only dangerous aspects of the hands, but also the stuff he could do on the more positive side, like the topiaries and the haircuts, which are his art.'

As shooting drew near, Tim Burton, who had cast Depp on the strength of his performance in *Cry-Baby* and had never seen *21*

Shear Perfection

During filming, Depp developed a close friendship not only with Tim Burton (who would later offer him the lead role in *Ed Wood*) but with Vincent Price. As well as advising Depp to buy art, the screen legend stayed in contact with the young actor after the film had wrapped and sent Depp a birthday message every year until his death.

Edward Scissorhands made its debut in Christmas 1990 and proved to be a comfortable critical and commercial success. A magnificent modern-day hybrid of *Pinnochio* and *Beauty and the Beast* worthy of the Brothers Grimm, the film opens in true 'once upon a time' fashion with the creation of Edward Scissorhands (Depp). Built by The Inventor (Vincent Price) who lived in a huge mansion high above town, Edward had virtually everything he needed to live – a heart, a brain and even a covering of skin. Everything, in fact, except a pair of hands. When the Inventor dies before he can give his 'son' the hands he had lovingly built for him, Edward is left with metal shears on each arm. Thus, his every act becomes potentially lethal, and Edward swiftly becomes scarred just from scratching his own face.

Edward lives alone in The Inventor's mansion until he is discovered by a kindly Avon lady, Peg Boggs (Dianne Wiest), who takes pity on him and invites the young man to stay with her family. Once in the suburb, Edward gains celebrity status thanks to his incredible hedge-cutting and hairdressing skills, and falls in love with Peg's daughter, Kim (Winona Ryder). However, Edward's fortunes change when he is framed for burglary by Kim's possessive boyfriend, Jim (Anthony Michael Hall) and accidentally wounds Peg's son, Kevin (Robert Oliver), with his scissorhands whilst saving him from being hit by a car. Realising that he has no future in the suburb, Edward returns to his mansion in a tear-jerking, snow-filled finale.

Edward Scissorhands is a true labour of love, and remains Tim Burton's finest and most personal film to date. In much the same way that director Steven Spielberg relived his childhood through *E.T. The Extra-Terrestrial*, *Edward Scissorhands* was the perfect vehicle for Tim Burton to explore his own feelings of isolation and eccentricity as an individual and as an artiste. The film is a visual and emotional treat, and Burton's extremely distinctive surreal imagery and unique outlook on the world have never been put to better use.

Although the entire cast of the film perform admirably, Depp dominates proceedings and delivers the most unusual and most unforgettable performance of his career. 'Although he has few lines, every

Above: Rejected by the outside world, Edward returns to his mansion alone

Left: Like a modern-day Romeo and Juliet, Edward and Kim (Winona Ryder) find themselves separated by circumstances

movement and every word is beautifully judged; the actor is particularly poignant during the scene in which he realises that he cannot touch the girl he loves, in case he tears her apart.

Depp handles the role with remarkable conviction and consequently received a much-deserved Golden Globe Award nomination for his inspired efforts.

During the first few weeks of the film's release, *Edward Scissorhands* soon became known as an emotionally-charged, guaranteed tear-jerker; Burton himself wept the first time he saw a complete cut of the film! The director later credited the film's leading man for its spell-binding power and impact: 'Johnny being as pure as he could be is the most important factor as to why the movie had such an emotional release,' he proudly stated.

Depp realised that he had contributed to something special when he saw the film for the first time at a cinema in California.

'When the audience first saw Edward they chuckled,' he said. 'Then they laughed. That made me a little nervous. But then they laughed in the all the right places and were really taken by the film. It was magic.'

5

DREAMERS, CLOWNS
AND GRAPES

Dreamers, Clowns
And Grapes

Above: Benny & Joon allowed Depp to play a romantic/comic lead opposite Mary Stuart Masterson

Opposite: To bring the character Sam to life, the actor studied the work of Charlie Chaplin, Harold Lloyd and Buster Keaton

help bid the unlikely horror anti-hero farewell, the actor agreed to make a brief, uncredited appearance and can be seen by eagle-eyed fans on a TV screen.

Several months later, Depp landed the lead role in *Arizona Dream,* a fantasy drama co-staring Oscar-winner Faye Dunaway (*Network, Bonnie and Clyde*) and veteran comedy star Jerry Lewis (*The Nutty Professor, The Bellboy*).

Filmed as *The Arrowtooth Waltz, Arizona Dream* follows the life of Axel Blackmar (Depp), a loveable simpleton haunted by visions of flying fish, Eskimos and Alaska. After an average night of heavy drinking, Axel learns that he has been kidnapped by his friend Paul (Vincent Gallo) and finds himself in Arizona.

Instead of returning to New York, Axel decides to stay in Arizona for a while and soon gets caught up in the dreams of those around him, including his Uncle Leo (Lewis), who asks him to be best man at his wedding and then take over his used car business; man-eating widow Elaine (Dunaway), who dreams of flying; and Elaine's troubled step-daughter Grace (Lili Taylor), who wishes to die and become a turtle.

As offbeat as they come, *Arizona Dream* proved to be a love-it-or-leave-it experience for critics and cinemagoers alike. Directed by Sarajevo's Emir Kusturica, the film is visually superb and boasts more than its fair share of stunning surreal (and sometimes symbolic) imagery, but is undermined by its silly and unsympathetic characters and, at two and a quarter hours, outstays it welcome by at least 30 minutes.

While Jerry Lewis and Faye Dunaway won widespread applause for their poignant and potty performances, critics couldn't make up their minds whether Depp was understated or asleep in the lead.

Ironically, widespread dissatisfaction with the film's downbeat ending (in which Axel abandons his dreams to return to reality) must have encouraged him to make the whimsical and uplifting romantic comedy

Don Juan De Marco (which extols the virtues of placing fiction over fact) three years later.

Although *Arizona Dream* sadly emerged as a box office flop, Depp found working on the film immensely enjoyable and so decided to stay with the offbeat for his next film, *Benny & Joon.*

Best described as a dysfunctional love story, *Benny & Joon* was the brainchild of screenwriter and former circus clown Barry Berman. Berman conceived the film as a romantic tribute to his favourite comedy stars, Buster Keaton and Charlie Chaplin, and incorporated elements of their renowned slapstick into the script.

Canadian-born director Jeremiah Chechik (*National Lampoon's Christmas Vacation*) perceived *Benny & Joon* as 'a romance between two oddities who fall in love' and felt that the movie would have a universal appeal 'because every human heart contains the potential for both pain and pleasure.'

When it came to casting the film's lead roles, Chechik's first choice to play Sam, an eccentric Chaplinesque drifter who manages to unintentionally bring love, despair and comedy into the lives of Benny and Joon, was Johnny Depp. The director had seen the actor in *Edward Scissorhands* and swiftly became intrigued by the possibility of working with him.

'When I first met with Johnny to discuss *Benny & Joon,* I began to understand how much he had brought to the role of *Edward Scissorhands,*' he explained. 'He is so emotionally expressive, doing what seems to be so little. It was clear that he would bring a thoroughly original and exciting energy to the role of Sam.'

Co-producer Donna Roth needed little persuasion to support Chechik's choice: 'There is something magical about Johnny, there is no doubt about it,' she stated. 'The first time we met him, it was like meeting a blind date at the front door and discovering, "My god, he is so wonderful". Johnny exceeded all of our expectations.'

For Depp, the most appealing aspect of starring in the film was the chance to recreate the comic magic of Chaplin, Keaton and Harold Lloyd and introduce it to a new generation of cinemagoers. The actor, who ironically had just lost the lead role in Richard Attenborough's biopic *Chaplin* to Robert Downey Jr, because his rival looked more like the screen legend than he did, studied videos of the great comedians and was subsequently coached and choreographed by mime, magician and silent film buff Dan Kamin – shortly after Kamin had completed supervising Downey's performance in *Chaplin!*

'I had such a great time rediscovering Keaton, Chaplin and Harold Lloyd,' said Depp. 'Comedy, especially when it is so physical, is extremely demanding. I developed an even greater respect for those guys as I began to try to do what they had accomplished in such a seemingly effortless way.'

Kamin was extremely impressed by Depp's work: 'The subtle movements are the hardest to capture, but Johnny did an incredibly marvellous job,' he gushed. 'He was really courageous and worked hard – even at the small things.'

As Depp laboured at perfecting Sam's slapstick, Mary Stuart Masterson (*Some Kind of Wonderful, Fried Green Tomatoes at the Whistlestop Cafe, Chances Are*) was cast as the love of his life, the mentally-retarded painter, poet and pyromaniac Joon, and Aidan Quinn (*Desperately Seeking Susan, Stake Out,*) assumed the role of Joon's over-protective brother, Benny.

During the two weeks prior to the start of shooting, Chechik gathered the film's leading cast members together to allow them to discuss their roles and rehearse their most pivotal scenes.

'It was important for me to create an atmosphere where the actors didn't feel at all inhibited about experimenting with ideas and contributing to the process,' the director explained. 'At the outset, I established very specific parameters for the story and its

Depp continued his exploration of the eccentric in his role as Gilbert in *What's Eating Gilbert Grape*

characters, but then, as rehearsals progressed, it started to become a mutual journey of discovery.'

Benny & Joon was shot on location in Spokane, Washington, during the summer of 1992 and was subsequently released in spring 1993, when it received strong reviews and became a minor box office hit.

Boasting a witty and inventive screenplay and excellent performances from a sterling cast, the film ultimately provides a

stunning showcase for Depp, who gives a performance which frequently ranks alongside his work in *Edward Scissorhands*. If the actor was seeking consolation for losing the lead role in *Chaplin*, then *Benny & Joon* was clearly the perfect vehicle for him; Depp excels at depicting Sam's Chaplinesque comedy and in one scene, successfully recreates Chaplin's famous dancing-bread-rolls sequence, which is also performed by Robert Downey, Jr in Attenborough's biopic!

which he stars as Gilbert Grape, a young grocery clerk who longs to leave his small Iowa town, Endora, but must stay and take care of his mentally-retarded brother, Arnie (Leonardo Di Caprio), his two troubled sisters, Amy (Laura Harrington) and Ellen (Mary Kate Schellhardt), and their obese mother (Darlene Cates). When Becky (Juliette Lewis) enters his hometown and his life, Gilbert decides that the time has come for him to take control of his life and dreams.

Directed with warmth and sensitivity by Sweden's Lasse Hallstrom (My Life As a Dog), *What's Eating Gilbert Grape* is a touching and charming tale, distinguished by some remarkable performances from its impressive cast.

As Gilbert Grape, a troubled beacon of sanity in a quirky world, Depp delivers a textured and thoughtful performance (which earned the actor his second Golden Globe Award nomination) whilst Leonardo Di Caprio is outstanding in the more demonstrative (and therefore, more obvious) role of Arnie, and was nominated for an Oscar for best supporting actor. Juliette Lewis delightfully rounds off the trio of talented young performers as the film's love interest, Becky.

When Johnny Depp first read the film's script, he agreed to take the lead role on the strength of its message. 'We tend to judge people harshly based on their appearance, whether they're overweight, ugly, handicapped or mentally challenged,' he said. 'Sometimes these people are looked on as freaks because they're different. What this film is saying is that they're human, like everyone else.'

Upon joining the film's cast and crew on location in Austin, Texas, Depp's first task was to build a believable screen relationship with Leonardo Di Caprio. As Di Caprio pointed out, 'We had a brotherly relationship on camera, so we had to be buddy-buddy with each other.'

During shooting, Depp's fascination with unusual foreign phrases and unusual smells came to the fore. He learned a number of

Top and centre: **Gilbert's relationship with his mentally-retarded brother Arnie (Leonardo Di Caprio) is fraught with incident**

Above: **Gilbert finds love and the hope of a new life with Becky (Juliette Lewis)**

Whilst discussing his latest unconventional role, Depp admitted that he felt a certain affinity with his offbeat roles: 'I feel like a bit of an oddball,' he explained, 'only because there's a lot of hate in the world – hate and greed – and I don't feel greedy and I don't hate too much, so I feel a bit freakish because of that.'

Depp continued his exploration of the eccentric in his next film, *What's Eating Gilbert Grape,* a quirky comedy/drama in

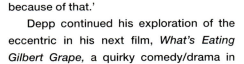

Dreamers, Clowns
And Grapes

'I don't think I was ever in love until I met Kate. I'm crazy about her.'

Above: Johnny demonstrates the fashion sense which has earned him the title of 'world's worst dressed man'

Opposite: Depp's relationship with supermodel Kate Moss is turbulent, even by his standards

strange Swedish phrases involving radishes from director Lasse Hallstrom and would enlist Di Caprio's aid in identifying the 150 smells typically found on a movie set.

'Johnny loved to see my facial expressions when I was disgusted by the smell of something gross, like decaying honeycomb, rotten eggs and pickled sausage,' remembers Di Caprio 'He'd give it to me to smell and I would do this gagging thing. In the end I couldn't stand it and charged him for the pleasure. I made about $500.'

Perhaps more significantly, however, Depp's four-year relationship with Winona Ryder came to an end during filming.

Although Depp felt that they had slowly drifted apart and that separating was the 'natural thing to do', it didn't make the situation any less painful for him. 'It was a really lonely time for me,' he explained. 'I poisoned myself constantly: drinking, didn't eat right, no sleep, lots of cigarettes.'

Ironically, Depp believed that his personal torment helped his on-screen performance. 'My feelings were close to the surface, so they were easy to manipulate,' he explained. 'I did feel lost at times and very confused about everything.'

Depp's problems were worsened by a series of press reports which claimed that he was romantically involved with co-star Juliette Lewis, and that their affair had resulted in Lewis' break-up with actor Brad Pitt. Lewis, however, has continually scoffed at all such reports. 'I was like, "Oh really – so soon?"'and the first time she read of her supposed liaison, she exclaimed 'We were only three weeks into the movie!'

Similarly, Depp was plagued with rumours about the appearance of his ill-fated tattoo pledging undying love to his former girlfriend – 'Winona Forever' Some reports claimed that it was removed a bit at

a time, so that at one point it read, 'Wino Forever'; one magazine suggested that it had been changed to 'Would You Forever?'; others simply said that it had been completely (and painfully) erased. In any case, Depp himself repeatedly refused to confirm or deny their stories.

If Depp had hoped that the tabloid press would leave him alone once the furore surrounding his break-up with Ryder was over, he was sadly mistaken. For as soon as he was spotted out on the town with British supermodel Kate Moss, the actor was back in the headlines.

The couple first met in a New York restaurant, when Moss was dining with friends of Depp. The actor joined the group and although 'there was no big thunderbolt' during their first encounter, they became an item shortly after.

They subsequently took a holiday in the Caribbean, where Depp presented her with a stunning diamond ring, signifying yet another engagement for the actor. After their break, Moss began signing autographs as 'Kate Moss Depp' and moved into his Hollywood home.Although Depp tried to reveal as little as possible about their relationship, he did state, 'I don't think I was ever in love until I met Kate. I'm crazy about her.'

Moss, meanwhile, repeatedly expressed her disbelief at dating one of the world's most popular heart-throbs: 'I've never felt anything like this before,' she said. 'I knew straight away that it was different.'

Despite their expressions of love and admiration, reports suggest that Depp's relationship with Moss has been a non-stop rollercoaster ride to put it mildly.

The couple have split up on several occasions, and so one can only guess whether or not the supermodel will ever become Mrs. 'Kate Moss Depp'.

6

THE WORLD'S WORST DIRECTOR

Tim Burton's affectionate biopic *Ed Wood* showcased Johnny Depp as Hollywood's famous cross-dressing, angora-loving film-maker

Thanks to a surprising series of roles in offbeat projects, as well as his off-screen, headline-grabbing antics, Johnny Depp had become widely known as the uncrowned king of quirk by 1993. It came as little suprise therefore when Disney announced that he was to play the part of Edward D. Wood, Jr, the infamous cross-dressing film-maker responsible for some of the worst films in the history of cinema, in *Ed Wood,* the affectionate biopic directed by Tim Burton.

Ed Wood was the brainchild of screenwriter/director Scott Alexander and screenwriter/journalist Larry Karaszewski, who first discussed the idea of making a biopic of Edward D. Wood, Jr, in the Eightie's, when they were freshman roommates at University of Southern California.

Following the success of their first collaboration, *Problem Child,* the pair met with the innovative producer/director Michael Lehmann (whose credits included *Heathers* and *Hudson Hawk*) in 1992 to outline their idea. Lehmann, a former schoolmate of Alexander and Karaszeski, fell in love with the idea and pitched it to Tim Burton and his production partner, Denise Di Novi.

The pair, who had just completed work on *Batman Returns*, felt that *Ed Wood* was the 'perfect vehicle' for them.

They commissioned Alexander and Karaszeski to write the script and soon secured the film's funding from Disney, who gave Burton a carte blanche to make the film. The director's first decision was to make the film entirely in black and white, and he soon dubbed *Ed Wood*: *The Player* meets *Twin Peaks*.

For Burton, the project had a particularly strong appeal. The visionary film-maker had grown up watching Ed Wood movies and slowly began to detect a 'poetic quality' and 'twisted form of integrity' in the way in which the so-called 'world's worst director' would not allow awful scripts, flimsy sets and frequently laughable acting to get in the way of his art. Furthermore, Burton felt a certain affinity with Wood; both directors were passionate about film-making; and Wood had built a professional and personal relationship with his childhood idol, horror icon Bela Lugosi, in much the same way that Burton had befriended Vincent Price.

Furthermore, it's hard to avoid the thought that had Tim Burton been working in the Fifties, his unorthodox output might well have been perceived by commercially-minded movie producers in a similar vein as Ed Wood's disasterpieces.

With funding and script ready to roll, Burton and Di Novi turned their attention to casting. Both film-makers were fully aware that the success of the project hinged on casting the correct actor in the title role, and agreed that Johnny Depp was the perfect choice to play the doomed director.

Depp was the first and only actor they ever seriously considered for the role: 'Ed Wood was extremely handsome and loveable, as is Johnny,' said Di Novi. 'But more importantly, Johnny is an actor who takes risks and gives unusual characters the special treatment and dignity they deserve.'

Below: **Johnny Depp as Edward D. Wood, Jr. – a man whose passion for film-making would not be tempered by his lack of talent**

The World's Worst Director

Top and centre: **Wood demonstrates his passion for angora sweaters**

Above: **Wood finds true love with Kathy (Patricia Arquette)**

When Tim Burton met with Depp to reveal his plans for the film, the actor was instantly intrigued. 'I thought it was an incredible idea,' he said. 'I immediately said, "Yes, yes, let's do it". I was already familiar with Wood's films, and I knew that nobody could tell his story better than Tim. Tim's passion became my passion.'

Depp's passion for the project proved essential in bringing *Ed Wood* to life. Due to the fact that there was little footage of Wood available (apart from his starring role in the semi-autobiographical sexual identity crisis movie *Glen or Glenda?* and a few brief silent clips of Wood directing), Depp had to rely on books and written material to get an idea of how to portray the legendary film-maker.

'I read whatever I could get my hands on, watched the films, and then put different people together in my brain,' the actor explained. 'I wanted to make him extremely optimistic, innocent, and a brilliant show-man all the same time. He was a man who loved making films. It was his whole life, and he didn't allow anything to discourage him.'

During the course of his research, Depp, like Tim Burton, developed an admiration for the much-maligned artist: 'Ed was someone who was not afraid to take chances and did exactlty what he wanted to do,' he enthused. 'He did the best that he could with what was available to him and was able to put together images that were surreal, with moments of genius, I think. His movies were all his and they were genuine. I hope Ed is remembered as an artist.'

Of course, what made *Ed Wood* a risky, and potentially embarrassing role for Depp was the director's penchant for women's clothes. Although Burton was aware of the potential pitfalls of the cross-dressing sequences, he felt confident that Depp could successfully manage to avoia them. 'People in drag are easy targets, but Johnny is so credible that he pulls it off without mak-ing it laughable,' he said. 'Besides, he really looks great in those clothes.'

Ironically, whilst studio executives were reported to have had cold-feet about the film's depiction of Wood's transvestite lifestyle, Depp wasn't bothered in the slight-est by the prospect of donning a blonde wig and *pink?* angora sweater.

'I considered it an experiment to see what it would be like to wear lots of women's accoutrements,' Depp stated. 'And I have to say I have a much deeper respect for women, and transvestites for that matter. I think Ed dressed in women's clothes because he really loved women and wanted to be closer to them.'

Costume designer Colleen Atwood, who had previously worked with Depp on *Edward Scissorhands,* was charged with the

Wood receives an offer he can't refuse in the re-creation of *Glen or Glenda?*

task of transforming the male heartthrob into a woman. Atwood was completely amazed by the finished result. 'Johnny looks great as a woman,' she said. 'The first time we put him in angora we were saying, "God, he looks really beautiful," even though the things weren't altered or fitted or anything.'

However, Depp's first impression of his drag act was somewhat different. 'When I first looked in the mirror, I thought I was the ugliest woman I had ever seen,' he said. 'I

mean, I looked absolutely huge in those clothes. Enormous!'

Besides charting Wood's life as a film-maker and transvestite, the film also explores the fascinating relationship between Wood and Bela Lugosi (Martin Landau); it shows with honesty and consideration how Lugosi helped Wood secure funding for some of his early projects whilst Wood helped revitalise the fading horror star's career in the final years of his life.

▶▶

The World's Worst Director

Above: A scene from Wood's most famous disasterpiece *Plan 9 from Outer Space*

Below: Wood directs fading horror superstar Bela Lugosi (Martin Landau)

'I see this film as a love story between two men,' said Landau. 'Ed and Bela really loved each other on a deep level. Sometimes Bela was like a father to Ed; sometimes Ed was like a father to Bela, and I think that Johnny and I have been able to recreate that sentimental bond between them.'

Ironically, the veteran performer inadvertently reminded the world of Depp's status as the natural successor to James Dean. The actor, who had known Dean at Lee Strasberg's renowned Actors Studio, said: 'Dean was a friend and I think Johnny is as close to Jimmy as anyone I've ever met.'

Depp found working with Landau to be straightforward and rewarding. 'Every scene we played together took on a life of its own and was more than just words on a page,' he said. 'My feelings were heartfelt and real.'

Ed Wood began shooting on 5 August 1993 and was filmed in various locations across downtown LA, as well as Torrance, Sierra Madre, Long Beach, Norwalk, Gardena and Eagle Rock. For one sequence of the movie, a section of the bustling Hollywood Boulevard was closed for several hours, whilst a mock-up of the legendary Brown Derby Hotel was constructed in the city's celebrated Ambassador Hotel.

Prinicipal photography of *Ed Wood* wrapped after nearly three and a half months of shooting, on 17 November.

According to Depp, *Ed Wood* was one of the happiest and smoothest shoots he had ever participated in. 'It was a very vibrant shoot,' the actor explained 'I mean, it was really tough. We were filming in some of the most claustrophobic, badly ventilated, most uncomfortable locations in Hollywood. My adrenaline was pumping all the way, but everyone from the ground up was giving 200 per cent. I think it has to be the most ensemble picture I've made.'

Patricia Arquette (who, like Depp started her career in a *Nightmare On Elm Street* movie), praised Depp's contribution to the on-set atmosphere: 'I think he energised everyone on set, he was as much a guiding force on the movie as Tim [Burton].'

During shooting, Depp received the ultimate accolade from Ed Wood's widow, Kathy, who told him that she was bowled over by his portrayal of her late husband and proceeded to give the actor Wood's wallet and phone book in order to provide an added touch of authenticity.

In its finished form, *Ed Wood* is an off-beat but highly entertaining tribute to the world's worst director. Based on Rudolph Grey's *The Life and Art of Edward D. Wood, Jr,* Burton's biopic begins in 1952, with the cross-dressing World War II hero and aspiring film-maker securing funding for his disastrous film debut, *Glen or Glenda?* Although the movie proves to be a critical and commercial disaster Wood is undeterred and desperately seeks funding for his second outing.

Over the course of a few months, Wood builds up an entourage of 'misfits and dope addicts', including Bela Lugosi (Martin Landau), would-be transsexual Bunny Breckinridge (Bill Murray), Swedish wrestler-turned-non-actor Tor Johnson (George 'The Animal' Steele), cult TV host Vampira (Lise Marie) and phoney psychic Criswell (Jeffrey Jones), all of whom help the artist finally bring his second film, *The Bride of the Monster*, to the screen. Shortly after the completion of the film, Wood's long suffering girlfriend

Dolores Fuller (Sarah Jessica Parker) walks out on him, but the director finds lasting love with his wife, Kathy (Patricia Arquette). Miraculously, *Ed Wood* ends on a triumphant note, with the Orson Welles-wanabee completing his self-confessed masterpiece, the infamous *Plan 9 From Outer Space*.

Although *Ed Wood* is clearly the work of a talented and visionary director, the film received a mixed critical reaction and ultimately provided Tim Burton (hitherto the master of surprise box office hits) with his first commercial catastrophe.

While no one dared suggest that Burton's film was worthy of the world's worst film-maker, many critics accused the film's depiction of Wood as a misunderstood artist in a cruel commercial world as being idealistic, naive and tiring.

Similarly, others condemned the way that the film glossed over many elements of Wood's life, such as his short-lived marriage to his first wife, Norma McCarty, his descent into alcoholism and the collapse of his career, when the director was forced to helm the infamous 'monster nudie pics' such as *Orgy of the Dead* and *The Cocktail Hostess.*

However, when viewed as an affectionate homage rather than definitive biopic, *Ed Wood* has much to offer. The film is absolutely littered with hilarious moments (most of which are based closely on fact!) and Tim Burton's loving recreation of Wood's 'classic' films are far more entertaining that the originals.

Perhaps best of all, though, Tim Burton manages to coax uniformly excellent performances from an impressive cast.

Johnny Depp isn't just superb as Ed Wood; he *is* Ed Wood. Manic, undefeatable and always sympathetic, it's a testimony to Depp's performance that the audience never laughs at him and really want him to find funding for his movie, even though they know he is doomed and would be better off giving up his career as a film-maker.

Depp also shows his flair for comedy, especially in the scene when he is faced with the charge of directing the worst film ever made. Undeterred by the criticism, Wood proudly states, 'My next one will be better'! Depp's work in *Ed Wood* won his third Golden Globe nomination for best actor.

Depp once again proves that he is not only an extremely gifted actor but a generous performer as well, by allowing his supporting cast their moments of glory.

Everyone, from Sarah Jessica Parker to Bill Murray, is well served by the movie, while Martin Landau gives the performance of his life as Bela Lugosi. Landau, a veteran performer whose previous roles in *Tucker: A Man and His Dream* and *Crimes and Misdemeanours* earned him two Oscar nominations, transforms himself into the late, great horror hero and consequently collected a well-earned Oscar for best supporting actor.

Despite its somewhat disastrous box office reception, Depp remained proud of *Ed Wood* and was delighted with its unique and authentic atmosphere. 'We have the essence of Wood's life as a film-maker and his relationship with Bela Lugosi,' he stated. 'This is homage. A real weird homage but nevertheless a respectful one. I hope everyone will see it that way.'

For Depp, however, the making of Ed Wood was marred by personal tragedy. Less than three weeks before the completion of principal photography, River Phoenix died of 'acute multiple drugs intoxication' (to quote Los Angeles county coroner Scott Carrier) on 31 October , in the Viper Room, the 'cool underground nightclub' on Sunset Strip co-owned by Johnny Depp. Depp was completely outraged by the way reporters transformed Phoenix's tragic death in to a media event.

'They were really disrespectful to him and to his memory, to his family, to his friends, to his fans,' said Depp 'The press was trying to tarnish his memory in the minds of all those people who loved him, when it all boils down to a very sweet guy who made a very big mistake, a fatal mistake, a mistake we're all capable of. I was really pissed off.'

Depp closed down the Viper Room for two weeks in order to allow Phoenix's fans to pay tribute to their idol and wait for the media attention to die down.

When he re-opened the club, the actor was pleased to report that all the 'gawkers' were nowhere to be seen and it had gone back to being 'a good place'.

Top: River Phoenix, who collapsed outside Johnny Depp's club, The Viper Room

Above: Fans pay tribute to River Phoenix by laying flowers on the pavement outside The Viper Room

7

THE WORLD'S
GREATEST LOVER

The World's Greatest Lover

Few cinemagoers had difficulty accepting Johnny Depp as the potentially-insane romantic hero Don Juan DeMarco

Above and opposite: Johnny Depp as Don Juan DeMarco – the world's greatest lover, or a first class story-teller?

Following the completion of *Ed Wood,* the announcement that Johnny Depp was set to star as a suave psychiatric patient who claims to be the world's greatest lover was greeted with instant applause and approval; after all, who would be better at playing an insane but irresistible individual than the so-called 'crazy heart-throb' Johnny Depp.

Originally entitled *Don Juan DeMarco and the Centerfold,* this seemingly tailor-made screen outing was written and directed by Jeremy Leven, a former therapist-turned-author, screenwriter and director. Inspired by Lord Byron's *Don Juan,* Leven thought of writing a whimsical romantic comedy which combined elements of Byron's classic novel with his own experience as a psychiatrist.

Leven subsequently wrote the film's script in a converted barn in Connecticut. By the time he had completed his screenplay, Leven had given the movie's casting little

▶▶

The World's Greatest
Lover

'The challenge for me was creating a character who was slightly cocky and noble, but likeable'

thought, but instead had become determined that his offbeat tale would mark his feature film directorial debut.

Once in Hollywood, Leven pitched *Don Juan DeMarco* as a $3 million romantic comedy and was delighted to hear that legendary film-maker Francis Ford Coppola (the winner of five Oscars, whose numerous credits include *Apocalypse Now* and the *Godfather* movies) had enjoyed the screenplay. Shortly after, Leven was shocked when Coppola signed on as producer, and told Leven that he was happy for him to direct.

Coppola was not the only one who was intrigued by Leven's concept. Upon reading his script, Johnny Depp expressed an interest in playing the film's title role. 'Jeremy's script was brilliant,' the actor enthused. 'It's incredible writing. The dialogue was so poetic and beautiful.'

Unsurprisingly, Leven felt that Depp was a perfect choice as the modern-day Don Juan, but was devastated to hear that the actor had one condition about taking the role: 'I was told Johnny wanted to do it, but that he'd only do if [Marlon] Brando played the psychiatrist,' the director explained. 'At that point, I thought the project was dead in the water, only to receive a second shock, hearing that Marlon was also interested.'

With the legendary Marlon Brando (*The Godfather, Last Tango In Paris, On The Waterfront*) and Depp in the film's leading roles, Leven's third casting coup came in the shape of Faye Dunaway, who signed on to play the film's female lead. As far as the actress was concerned, the main appeal of the project was working with both Marlon Brando and her former co-star in *Arizona Dream,* Johnny Depp.

'Marlon's an idol, a dream,' she said. 'He's a myth to every working actor in the world. And Johnny's a close second . . . Johnny's like the heir apparent.'

Thus, with Brando, Depp and Dunaway in the leading roles, *Don Juan De Marco* transformed from a low-budget comedy to a $20 million potential blockbuster.

Prior to the start of shooting, Depp developed Don Juan's Latino accent, which he based on Ricardo Montalban's distinctive tones in the long-running American romantic fantasy series, *Fantasy Island,* and also took a few fencing lessons for the film's pivotal fight scene.

'The challenge for me was creating a character who was slightly cocky and noble, but likeable,' he said. 'I needed to create someone who has a strong sense of himself but is still lost.'

Ironically, the film once again featured Depp in drag, during the scene in which Don Juan invades a harem. However, when asked if he would appear in drag in every film he made, the actor laughed, 'It's not a permanent trend.'

Besides bringing the Don Juan life, Depp also had to face the challenge of working opposite Brando. The young actor spoke to the living legend prior to visiting him at home for a meal. Fortunately, the experience wasn't half as terrifying as the young actor had imagined: 'I thought I was going to be freaked out, but he put me at ease instantly,' Depp confessed. 'He's just a guy, just a man, who happens to be incredibly gifted and brilliant.'

Depp spent the summer of 1994 shooting the film and found the best thing about the project was starring alongside Brando and Dunaway. 'They are both actors with incredible careers,' he said. 'I was privileged to work alongside them and learn.'

A whimsical and wonderful slice of romantic drama, *Don Juan DeMarco* opens with Dr. Jack Mickler (Brando) rushing to the aid of a young man (Depp) about to commit suicide. Masked, cloaked and brandishing a

Top: Don Juan is sold as a slave in the Middle East

Above: Dr. Jack Mickler (Marlon Brando) is captivated by Don Juan's claims

Opposite: Don Juan prepares to fight his father's killer

The World's Greatest Lover

Top: **Depp with former financee Winona Ryder**

Above: **Kate Moss poses with her on/off boyfriend**

Below: **Both Depp and Juliette Lewis denied rumours of a romance**

sword, the 21-year-old claims to be Don Juan, the world's greatest lover. Although Don Juan is devastated at the loss of his one true love, Dona Ana (Geraldine Pailhas), Mickler manages to convince him not to end his life, and the man is promptly taken into police custody.

Don Juan is subsequently committed and assigned to Mickler, a highly respected but burnt-out physician. With only ten days to go before his retirement, Mickler becomes enthralled by the young man's poetic tales of romance and adventure, and begins to re-evaluate several elements of his own life, including his relationship with his wife, Marilyn (Faye Dunaway). While all the evidence suggests that the young man is in fact a dreamer, Bickler gradually accepts him as the legendary lover, Don Juan.

Thus, *Don Juan DeMarco* is a heart-warming, charming and uplifting tale about the triumph of fantasy over reality. Although director Leven ultimately fails to give his contemporary fairy tale the lasting impact it so obviously strives for (unlike the unforgettable *Edward Scissorhands*), he ensures that the film never has a dull moment and allows its contrasting leading men to deliver extremely admirable and surprisingly complementary performances.

Top-billed Marlon Brando is an utter delight as Mickler and oozes charisma, but never allows himself to overwhelm his

co-stars. Depp matches the screen legend in the film's most challenging role and is simply faultess; whilst many actors would be laughable, unsympathetic or unappealing, Depp avoids the pitfalls of his role and performs with admirable conviction throughout.

Given the apparent ease with which Depp delivered such lines as, 'I give women pleasure if they desire it – of course it is the greatest pleasure they will ever experience,' members of the public inevitably began to wonder if in fact the oft-engaged heart-throb wasn't acting. The actor once revealed: 'There's such confidence about Don, and I can relate to that. But at the same time, it's so foreign to me that it's funny. I mean, a guy who says, "I am the world's greatest lover". I'd be too embarrassed to go up to a girl and say stuff like that.'

Regardless of how true to life Depp's performance was, it did nevertheless lead to the actor being voted as the 'sexiest star of all time' by *Empire*. Described as 'enigmatic' by the leading film magazine, Depp beat such all-time greats as Marilyn Monroe, Michelle Pfeiifer, Robert Redford, Grace Kelly, Brigitte Bardot, Sean Connery, Paul Newman, Mel Gibson, James Dean and Tom Cruise to the title, and defeated his contemporaries Keanu Reeves (who ranked 17th) and Brad Pitt (23rd). Depp also claimed the prize for the 'sexiest legs' in screen history!

Don Juan DeMarco was released at the beginning of 1995 and proved to be a modest international box office hit. However, Depp was proud to report that neither the film nor the role changed his lifestyle.

As the movie hit cinemas around the world, Depp hit the headlines for being charged with vandalising a $10,000 room at the distinguished Mark Hotel in New York. The actor later explained that he was reacting to a 'wild dog that jumped out of the closet at me'. Ever since, Depp (who often stays at hotels under the alias of 'Mr Stench') has noticed that hoteliers 'tend to look a bit nervous' whenever he stays at their establishments!

8

TIME FOR ACTION

Time For Action

Nick of Time marked Depp's debut as an action hero

Above and opposite: **The wrong man at the wrong place at the wrong time – mild-mannered accountant Gene Watson (Depp)**

material he was offered. 'I hate the obvious stuff,' Depp often stated. 'I just don't respond to it. I get a bad feeling from it.'

Depp therefore declined the lead roles in the high-profile blockbusters *Legends of the Fall* (the sweeping melodrama which scored another critical and commercial hit for Brad Pitt) and *Speed* (the high-octane actioner which consolidated Keanu Reeves' position as an international superstar). The actor also turned down multi-million dollar offers to appear in the teen-orientated adaptation of *The Three Musketeers* and the Sharon Stone disaster, *Sliver.*

However, just prior to starting work on the film *Ed Wood* in 1993, Depp realised that he was starting to become typecast in off-beat roles and began to ponder a different path for his career. 'Maybe I've done enough of this wearing-my-art-on-my-sleeve stuff, maybe I've played all the pure-hearted, vulnerable oddballs that I should do. Maybe it's time to enter into another acting arena altogether because I don't want to wind up just repeating myself.'

By the time he had finished work on *Don Juan DeMarco,* the following year, Depp felt confident that he would not have to compromise his art to star in an occasional blockbuster and had considered the possibility that starring in box office hits might allow him greater leverage in the creation and development of films.

'If there's something good that has commercial potential, I would be ready to dive into it,' revealed Depp. Shortly after, Depp signed up to star in *Nick of Time*, an action-thriller directed by John Badham, whose credits include such financial smashes as *Saturday Night Fever, Stakeout, Bird on A Wire* and *WarGames.*

In the years following *21 Jump Street,* Johnny Depp repeatedly declined lucrative offers to star in big-budget, highly commercial projects (the so-called 'sure-fire hits') and instead chose to appear in a series of small-scale, quirky labours of love.

Upon leaving the popular TV series, the actor made it clear that he hated being an American media sensation and had no desire to trade his teen-idol tag for international movie superstardom.

'Tom Cruise is the biggest box office star in the world,' remarked Depp, 'and I don't think I could be that . . . I'm not ambitious in that way at all.'

During the early part of the Nineties, Depp's idiosyncratic film choices enabled him to abandon the teen idol tag which he abhorred and gave him time to develop his own inestimable acting talents.

Furthermore, the actor invariably found the more offbeat and unusual projects more interesting than the more conventional

Top: Depp leaps into action in his most commercial project to date

Above: The actor confers with *Nick of Time*'s veteran director John Badham

A twist on the theme of an ordinary man being caught at the wrong place at the wrong time, *Nick of Time* opens with accountant Gene Watson (Depp) and his six-year-old daughter Lynn (Courtney Chase) being taken hostage by two terrorists posing as police officers, Mr. Smith (Christopher Walken) and Ms. Jones (Roma Maffia).

Mr Smith tells Watson that he has 80 minutes to kill the liberal California State governor Eleanor Grant (Marsha Mason); should he fail or warn the authorities, the accountant's daughter will be killed. To make matters worse, the terrorists have already arranged to pin the blame of the murder on Watson and have planted evidence which depicts him as a deranged loner bent on revenge.

When *Nick of Time* was given the green light by Paramount, the studio executives expected that accountant-turned-reluctant hero Gene Watson would be taken by an established action hero, such as Mel Gibson

or Bruce Willis. However, executive producer D. J. Caruso always felt that the film would work better if the lead role was played by an actor who is not associated with action-man heroics by the audience. Consequently, from the moment Johnny Depp was suggested to play the role, Caruso felt that he was a perfect choice.

'Because his role in *Nick of Time* is very different from what we've seen Johnny do in the past,' said Caruso, 'the audience will be rooting for him even as they wonder whether he can be the hero.'

Although the executives at Paramount expected Depp to instantly decline the chance to star in *Nick of Time,* the actor became intrigued when he learned that the film would take place in 'actual time'; in other words, cinemagoers would stay with Gene Watson throughout the 80 minutes he is given to kill the governor.

He then became interested in the possibility of transforming the film's lead character, Gene Watson, from a mild-mannered accountant into a courageous hero. As Depp pointed out, 'Gene goes from one extreme to another – from one emotion to the next – in the fraction of a second.'

Nick of Time began shooting on 2 April 1995 and wrapped 19 June. Whilst the majority of filming took place in the Westin Bonaventure Hotel (the largest convention hotel in Los Angeles), the remaining sequences of the movie were shot in LA's Union Station and in the famous Paramount studio lot. *Nick of Time* was shot largely in sequence in order to allow Depp to capture his character's development during his 80 minute ordeal, and John Badham directed the movie in an unglamorous, straightforward and 'quasi-documentary' style.

'Our film was shot as if we just happened upon these people and their circumstances,' said Badham. 'The actors were filmed without make-up using hand-held cameras to achieve a raw, realistic feeling.'

For Depp, shooting *Nick of Time* proved to be an unusual and highly rewarding experience. 'We did a lot of scenes that involved two or three cameras, which reduced the number of takes and kept a freshness and spontaneity to the acting,' the actor explained. 'You're not bound within frame lines and really feel like you can go anywhere and do anything.'

Unlike some of his earlier projects, the actor found it easy to relate to his character's situation and dilemma: 'To play the role I drew on what's accessible, and family is very important to me,' he stated. 'I have nieces and nephews that I absolutely worship. If anything ever happened to them, I would go crazy and do anything to save them.'

Besides marking his long-awaited foray into the world of the big-budget blockbuster, *Nick of Time* also marked Depp's debut as an action hero – albeit a reluctant and unlikely one. Depp felt it was essential that he did as much of his own stuntwork as possible, in order to capture his character's unease and increasing desperation in his action-man antics. As a result, the actor performed around 90 per cent of his own stunts, including a 90 foot fall.

Prior to its winter 1995 release, *Nick of Time* was widely tipped as a box office hit

and was expected to emulate the surprise success of *Speed* the previous year. In an insensitive (and supremely stupid) move, the thriller was released in America on November 22, the anniversary of President John F. Kennedy's assassination.

Unsurprisingly, few cinemagoers went to see the film in its all-important opening weekend, and the movie was swiftly yanked out of theatres to make room for such smashes as *Toy Story*, *Jumanji* and *Father of the Bride Part II*.

However, despite its poor reception, *Nick of Time* remains an above average and mildly entertaining thriller. While the film is riddled with plot holes and never comes close to fulfilling the promise of its brilliantly paranoid premise, John Badham builds the suspense quite nicely and delivers the occasional chill amongst the impressive thrills.

In the most conventional role of his post-*Jump Street* career, Johnny Depp is totally convincing as the ordinary man who becomes the victim of extraordinary circumstance; the only thing remarkable about his performance is just how unremarkable it is!

Although he is painfully believable in the scenes in which he confronts the prospect of committing a murder against his will, Depp's role as an 'everyman' character never really utilises his unique talent as a performer and the actor frequently seems wasted – at times, he becomes so 'low-key' and 'ordinary' that he looks set to disappear from the screen altogether.

With Depp constrained by the normality of his character and most of the cast never managing to elevate themselves beyond caricature status, Christopher Walken tends to dominate proceedings as the film's cold-hearted villain, Mr Smith.

Thus, whilst *Nick of Time* was far from a complete artistic failure, if it was meant to move Johnny Depp into the superstar bracket (a la Keanu Reeves in *Speed*) it was nothing short of a disaster. It is, however, ironic that just as Keanu has repeatedly failed to win the critical acclaim he seeks in such uncommercial films as *Little Buddha* and *My Own Private Idaho,* Depp has discovered that universal acclaim and admiration does not necessarily convert into big box office revenue.

Top: Watson is given his instructions by the sinister Mr Smith (Christopher Walken)

Above: Watson must kill California State govenor Eleanor Grant (Marsha Mason) to save his daughter's life

9

DEEPLY DEPPY

Deeply Deppy

A unique and unpredictable screen talent, Johnny Depp looks set to captivate moviegoers for decades to come

Above and opposite: **Accountant William Blake (Johnny Depp) becomes an unlikely legend in the contemporary western** *Dead Man*

Johnny Depp has never been more popular – or busier. Despite his reluctance to star in potential blockbusters which could transform him into an international superstar and line both his own pockets and those of film studio executives, the actor claims a modest (by Hollywood terms) $4 million per movie and continues to make unpredictable, eclectic and inspired film choices.

Depp is often considered for a range of roles that more conventional stars, such as his leading rivals Brad Pitt and Keanu Reeves, can only dream of and, more often than not, he manages to deliver unique and remarkable perfomances.

As a result, Depp is totally unconcerned by the fact that he hasn't broken into the commercially-driven mainstream movie-making, or that he is lagging behind Keanu and Brad in the 'bankability' stakes.

If stardom and money had been his only goals, Depp would have taken the easy option at the beginning of the Nineties and used his 'teen heart-throb' and 'proto-James Dean' tags to launch him into a number of films designed to emulate the success of *21 Jump Street*.

Instead, he has managed to successfully redefine his screen image with a series of offbeat roles in eclectic, uncommercial projects which the actor himself found personally appealing.

Although Depp's new screen persona, coupled with his equally unpredictable screen antics, won him the new tag of 'odd-ball heart-throb', it also brought the actor widespread acclaim, praise and popularity.

Regardless of his allergy to 'popcorn pictures', film-makers and moviegoers alike continue to go Deeply Deppy over Johnny Depp. In keeping with his eclectic film choices, Depp's most recent projects include *Dead Man*, a contemporary western

directed by cult filmmaker Jim Jarmusch (*Stranger Than Paradise, Down By Law, Mystery Train*). Shot in black and white, *Dead Man* traces the spiritual journey of William Blake (Depp), a Cleveland accountant who becomes an unlikely legend when

he is accused of murder and subsequently flees into the American wilderness accompanied by an Indian.

When asked about the appeal of starring in yet another uncommercial cult classic, the actor replied: 'Would you say no to a cowboy

▶▶

Deeply Deppy

'I still feel like I'm this seventeen-year-old gas station attendant in South Florida.'

Above: Divine Rapture, the Irish comedy which reunited Depp with Marlon Brando, was scrapped when the film's financing collapsed a mere ten days into production

Above: Donnie Brasco pairs Depp with another *Godfather* star, Al Pacino

movie in black and white and co-stars like Gabriel Byrne, John Hurt, Alfred Molina and Robert Mithcum and music by Neil Young?'

Like any Hollywood star, Depp's name is constantly linked with upcoming films and projects, many of which the actor is completely unaware of.

Recent reports have suggested that Depp's future projects include the starring role in Warners' big-screen adaptation of the cartoon show *Speed Racer* directed by Julien Temple (*Absolute Beginners*), the title role in *Donnie Brasco*, in which he would co-star with *Godfather* legend Al Pacino, and a Scottish film entitled *The Cull*.

Depp has publicly confirmed his desire to star in *It Only Rains At Night,* an unusual drama directed by Neal Jimenez (*The Waterdance*). Shortly after reading the film's script, Depp said, 'When I first read *Edward Scissorhands,* I realised that such a film was only going to come around once; that I would never see it again. *It Only Rains At Night* is also like that.'

However, one film that cinemagoers are unlikely to see Depp in is *Divine Rapture*, the doomed Irish comedy in which the actor co-starred with Marlon Brando, Debra Winger and John Hurt. After only a mere ten days of shooting, production ceased on 24 July 1995, when the film's financing unmiraculously collapsed.

Looking ahead, Depp admits that his ideal projects would include movie adaptations of *Crime and Punishment* and *Richard III,* and that he would like to play the unfortunate hero of Kafka's *Metamorphosis* – the everyday tale of a man who is transformed into a giant waterbug!

Of Course, Depp has never been one to sit on his laurels and now looks set to make his directorial debut in *The Brave,* a $6 million movie based on the novel by Gregory McDonald.

As well as taking the helm of The Brave, he will also co-write the script (with his brother, D. P. Depp) and will also star in the 'highly-commercial' venture, which depicts

the life of a desperate Angeleno who accepts a part in a 'snuff' movie.

Despite the obvious pressure and risks, Depp is confident about his move into pastures new. 'Since I've worked with so many wonderful directors and I've sponged off of them and stolen as much as I can, I feel I'm ready to try it,' he said I might try it only once, but I should at least try it . . . If it fails, I can always go back to trying it as a rock musician.'

Although he hasn't abandoned the movie business for the rock 'n' roll industry quite just yet, Depp continues to play guitar on a part-time basis and his latest group is 'P', in which he plays alongside Gibby Haynes (of the Butthole Surfers), former-Sex Pistol Steve Jones, Bill Carter, Sal Jenco and Flea (of the Red Hot Chilli Peppers). At the beginning of 1996, 'P' began to work on their debut album.

Of course, Johnny Depp is well aware that he has come a long way since he arrived in Hollywood in 1984 to pursue a career as a musician. Reviewing his work, the actor concedes that he has played more than his fair share of unconventional roles.

'There seems to be a constant theme in things I do which deal with people who are considered 'freaks' by so-called 'normal' people,' he said. 'I guess I'm attracted to these off-beat roles because my life's been a bit abnormal.'

The actor also points out that these supposedly eccentric choices have allowed him to work with some of the world's finest and most renowned film directors. 'For all of them, it's impossible to compromise,' he explained, 'and that makes it much easier for me to work with them.'

Depp is equally aware that he is as famous for his remarkable body of work as he is for his chequered love life and wild antics. The actor jokes that the media have romantically linked him with everyone from the Pope to the Queen of England, and that he isn't the 'unstoppable ladies' man' that the press portray him as.

'When you're growing up, you go through a series of misjudgements,' he explained. 'We all mess up. Part of it is just being young, and I was really young for the longest time. My relationships weren't as heavy as people think they were.'

Despite a string of finite romances, the actor believes in 'a society where people don't get divorced every five minutes: you can stay married for 75 years. It's been done and it's beautiful. When I see people celebrating their 75th wedding anniversary I want to study them. It's incredible.'

Depp has also made it clear that he is not a thirtysomething teenage tearaway and that he questions some of his earlier actions, including his celebrated love of tattooing.

'It's a stupid thing to do, I realise that,' he said 'I haven't done it in a few years . . . No, don't do this one at home, kids.'

However, Depp believes that he personally has been blissfully unaffected by stardom, fame and money. 'I still feel like I'm this seventeen-year-old gas station attendant in South Florida,' he once explained 'and that it's other people who place this strange stigma on you.'

Not surprisingly, the musician-turned-actor-turned-writer/director believes that if his showbusiness career was to suddenly evaporate, he could be just as happy making a living as a gardener.

Depp also claims his long-term plans have remained constant and that he has always wanted to 'get married, have kids, a couple of goldfish, lawnmower, asphalt driveway, eat doughnuts in the morning.'

However, if that scenario sounds a bit too domesticated for one of the world's most eccentric stars, rest assured that a conventional future for Johnny Depp is highly unlikely: 'Part of me wants to walk a dog and change a diaper,' he laughs, 'and the other part wants to go and eat dirt somewhere!'

Will Kate Moss be sharing Johnny Depp's life when he changes diapers, walks the dog and eats dirt?

▶▶

Johnny Depp

1984	*A Nightmare on Elm Street*
1985	*Private Resort*
1986	*Slow Burn* (Cable TV Movie)
	Platoon
1990	*Cry-Baby*
	Edward Scissorhands
1991	*Freddy's Dead: The Final Nightmare*
1992	*Arizona Dream*
1993	*Benny & Joon*
	What's Eating Gilbert Grape
1994	*Ed Wood*
1995	*Don Juan DeMarco*
	Nick of Time
1996	*Dead Man*

Plus:

1987 - 1990 The TV show *21 Jump Street* (4 seasons)

▶▶

▶▶